Look After Your Bones

Emma Kleinhans

BookLeaf
Publishing

Presentation by *BookLeaf Publishing*

Web: www.bookleafpub.com

E-mail: info@bookleafpub.com

ISBN: 978-93-95784-31-3

First edition 2022

DEDICATION

For the twins

ACKNOWLEDGEMENT

Thanks to my mum, for emotional and financial support.

PREFACE

This collection of poetry was written by
somebody that has never written poetry before,
so go easy on me. It was inspired by nature,
music and art. From short haikus to narrative
poems, this is a collection of thoughts and
feelings that I didn't know I had in me.

Flower

A flower, so sweet
A whiff of perfume on wind
Captivates the bee

No Rules

There is no rule in the world, that I must obey
I do what I want, to their dismay
No law, no regulation, no directive
An agent of chaos, from their perspective
Every command, I ignore
Give me an order, I withdraw
For I am a creature that can't be constrained
I am a cat, my human well trained.

Look After Your Bones

Look after your bones, they live forever
Cut me wide open, flay the flesh away
When the skin suit's sloughed, all that's left is
bone
Muscle and tendon, no reason to stay.

My bones have wandered, a great escapade
To drift aimlessly, in ocean currents
Polished by the sand, rounded at the edge
Forth and back and forth, with no more
judgements.

Gale winds turn my bones, to dust on the wind
Particles floating, to places unknown
Drift and swirl and curl, the freedom brings hope
Minerals of talc, on the breeze I roam.

Rain soaking through dirt, right down through
the ground
To a troubled heart, guarded by a cage
A calcified cage, chilled right to the bone
Dampening the shroud, cold rain soothes the
rage.

The illiac crest, an empty bird's nest
The right conditions, bone is petrified
A sedimental, a sentimental
An immortal grave, at once fossilized.

Love

Love is a fiery blaze...

NO. STOP IT.

Love is not a fire. Fires burn.
Fires consume and destroy.

Love is comfort.
Love is content, calm, complaisant.
Love is when everything just "fits".

Love is putting the last piece in a jigsaw puzzle.
Love is always having the correct change.
Love is when you have exactly the right amount
of sugar left to make a cake.
Love is a warm bowl of soup on a cold day.
Love is not eating the last peach, because you
know how much your partner loves peaches.
Love is when they hate pickles and you love
pickles, so you get to eat theirs.

Love shouldn't burn. It shouldn't hurt.
Love should be a cool breeze to soothe the fiery
heat.

Medusa

Surrounded by grey pillars, stalagmites
She sits among them
With their gleeful, lustful faces
They died to glimpse her
They would have traded anything to touch her
But never would another man
Even if it were possible, she wouldn't let them
They'd never get closer than her spearpoint
But Athena made sure she wouldn't need
weapons
Just a glimpse of her beauty
Would stone them to death

She wandered, searching for something
So many times her heart was broken
She figured she may as well go see her
It was too painful to be on this earth
Her last image imprinted in her mind
Would be of the greatest beauty
Entering the mouth of the cave
She heard a resentful sigh
Their eyes met

She froze, stone cold still
While every past life fell away
"I haven't seen one like you here before"
She said as she slithered closer
Her bemusement as the girl blinked her eyes
Why was this one immune?

"From now on and forever, any man who gazes
upon you, will be turned into stone"
Athena's curse, her permanent solitude

"Ah, but she is no man"

The girl came closer, her troubles forgotten
"I came here to die, instead I fell in love".

Depression

I feel so alone
always depressed
sad down to the bone
tired and can't get any rest.

Always on my own
feeling so oppressed
mind is a war zone
body is always stressed.

I get no relief
so I'll sink with my teeth
into alcohol, drugs and the rest.

No Mercy

When they make you sell your hair and teeth
Give no quarter
As they strip your meat from your bones
Give no quarter

When they take pieces of your soul
Have no mercy
Take your pride and joy
Have no mercy

They will try to destroy you
They will try to dim your light
Don't let them
Be fierce, be relentless
Use your power to bring them down.

How It Feels To Die

To live with chronic illness
is waiting in the stillness
a mind full of distress
feeling like a grim mess.

It feels like dying slowly
Grim Reaper breathes quite closely
not strong enough to live wholly
should I turn to the Holy?

The pain is spreading
the water I'm treading
insides are shredding
I'm stressing.

This life is a painful existence
but from a distance
they see only my persistence
not my need for assistance.

I'm only half of sixty
so why am I sufficiently
inundated medically
it's such a brutality.

This is how it feels
when my body will not heal
my will to live it steals
my weakness it reveals.

The burden of being chronically ill
the pain I want to kill
it cannot be fixed with a pill
especially not positive will.

This dreadful pain
is a mental chain
around my brain.
A devil's stain.

I Fell

I'm sorry that I fell in love with you
I promise that I really didn't mean to
But when I look at your eyes so warm
Friend or lover? I'm torn.

I can't stop staring at him
From his hands to his lips
From his lips to his hips
I want them pressed to my skin.

I didn't mean to fall in love with you
Despite my reluctance, love grew
All I wanted was a friend
In my dreams, I'll just pretend.

A Terrible Choice

Depression has two paths.

You either suffer in silence,
or you make others suffer in your place.

Injustice

Injustice is rife
in the world today
for children to eat
they must work all day

Black kids are shot down
by a blue dressed clown
just buying candy
and walking through town

Women die in back alleys
despite the rallies
because old white men
like to control them

Indigenous people
they go missing
but nobody looks
barely noticing

Gays and trans people
get bullied and beat
the hate so vile
can't walk down the street

Men die by the batch
commit suicide
they can't see their kids
the mothers, they lied

Animals aren't here
to race to the death
exploited for cash
until their last breath

When the president
and prime minister
get to decide
which one of us lives
and which of us dies

When injustice is rife
that's when we uprise.

Club Foot

Born with ugly feet
Bruised like I've been beat
Swollen up with lumps
Everyday new bumps

Born with twisted bones
Walking on the stones
Feet don't fit the mold
Over pain threshold

Born with crooked toes
My limping it shows
Covered with long scars
It hurts, I see stars

Born with horrid pain
Surgery in vain
Walking is caput
Born with a club foot

Marilyn

Unwanted as a child,
wanted by everyone as an adult,
but your beauty was only a small part of you.

Your mind was greater than they ever knew.
Too smart for your own good,
but not smart enough to not let yourself get used.

All you wanted was to be loved,
but they loved to have you on their arm,
as an ornament, a trophy to show off.

They used you to make money
and left you broken.
Addiction and sadness
is a deadly combination.

Always playing a part,
because you thought no one would love the real
you,
but your light forever shines.
You are loved, Norma Jeane.

Mother Nature

We are killing Mother Nature
We have put her life in danger
Heat is rising southern neighbour
Time to call an undertaker

Made by a sculptor, a painter
But destined to suffer later
Duck, take cover, there is danger
Treat her like an utter stranger

We have made her suffer major
If she was a thunder maker
Strike us down, a hunter, slayer
Send us to the upper chamber

Life

Into dirt
A seed underground
Roots like veins
Small stem reaching for sunlight
Cotyledons
First true leaves
Translucent leaves
Midrib and veins
Breathing oxygen
Water droplets and sunlight
Make flowers bud
Velvet soft petals
Velvet soft colours
Sticky stamens
Attract pollination
Fruit so sweet
Drops when overripe
Into dirt
A seed underground

Grief

Grief is strange

You can lose a loved one
and feel completely numb.
Then you beat yourself up
for not feeling enough.
Hate yourself
because you're not as sad as everybody else.

And then two years later
you break down in the supermarket
because it just hit you
that they are gone.
If you push the grief down long enough
it will explode when you least expect it.
And it will feel fresh all over again.

You wake up in the morning
and for those first few minutes
you don't remember.
And then it hits you
like a gut punch.
They're not coming back.
And so you live their death again
every morning.

They say grief gets lesser every day
but mine grows bigger one day
and smaller the next.
I never know whether it will sting like a paper
cut
or feel like a dagger in the heart.
I just know it's here to stay.

Thoughts

Depression is real
It can tear you to pieces
With a single thought

Real Girl

I wish I was a real girl
Just a normal school girl
Pretty with her hair curled
Do a little skirt twirl

Pretend I am a real girl
Not a troubled fool girl
Uncontrolled brain whirl
Crazy little wisdom pearl

More Thoughts

It's hard to find anything of worth
In this mind of mine
Every thought I roll around in my head
Until they're as smooth as tumbled stones
Even though I ruminate
The thoughts still seem so raw to me

I try to write pretty thoughts
But reading them back I feel unworthy
My conversation is lacking
Bored look on the faces of those I talk to
I wish my brain wasn't so confusing
Even I have trouble deciphering my meaning

Mental Illness

I need a break from life.
Give me a holiday in a padded room.
A getaway in an institution.
An asylum seems more hospitable than my life.

Mental illness is a cage.
More debilitating than most diseases.
Depression, anxiety, OCD, PTSD.
They rule my life and ruin it too.

Too depressed to leave the house.
Too anxious to sleep.
Too obsessed to enjoy life.
Too stressed to relax.

I have to find a reason to live.
If I want to survive this life.

Animals

I get along better with animals,
than I ever have with humans.
They erase all my troubles,
they have no illusions.

They don't care what you look like,
or how much money you make.
They are so childlike,
they can tell who is fake.

Animals are honest,
they love you unconditionally.
Give them what you promised,
and they'll love you especially.

Cat or dog, bird or horse
big or small, I love them all.
They'll be your company of course,
without them I withdrawal.